Chase, Wiggle, Chomp

TEACHING VERBS

BY LISA OWINGS

The Child's World®
childsworld.com

Published by The Child's World®
1980 Lookout Drive • Mankato, MN 56003-1705
800-599-READ • www.childsworld.com

ACKNOWLEDGMENTS
The Child's World®: Mary Swensen, Publishing Director
Red Line Editorial: Editorial direction and production
The Design Lab: Design

Photographs ©: Vitaly Titov & Maria Sidelnikova, cover, 2;
Shutterstock Images, 4, 5, 6-7, 13, 15; Guy J. Sagi/Shutterstock
Images, 9; Cristina Muraca/Shutterstock Images, 10-11; Sunny
Studio/Shutterstock Images, 12

ISBN 9781503808331
LCCN 2015958423

Printed in the United States of America
Mankato, MN
June, 2016
PA02304

ABOUT THE AUTHOR

Lisa Owings has a degree in English and
creative writing from the University of
Minnesota. She has written and edited a wide
variety of educational books for young people.
Lisa lives in Andover, Minnesota.

Verbs are words that show action. Look for **verbs** in this book. You will find them in **bold** type.

Tasha **walks** her dog, Rio. Rio **chases** a squirrel! He **pulls** Tasha behind him.

Milo **watches** a caterpillar **eat** a leaf. The caterpillar **wiggles**. It will **build** a cocoon and **transform** into a moth!

7

Ella **sees** a fawn **chomping** on grass. Ella **stands** still. The fawn might **be** scared and **run** away.

Ari **plays** and **laughs** with his friends. They **bounce, throw,** and **kick** balls.

Jess **reads** about sailing. She **imagines** being a sea captain. Jess **goes** boating with her dad. He **drives** the boat fast!

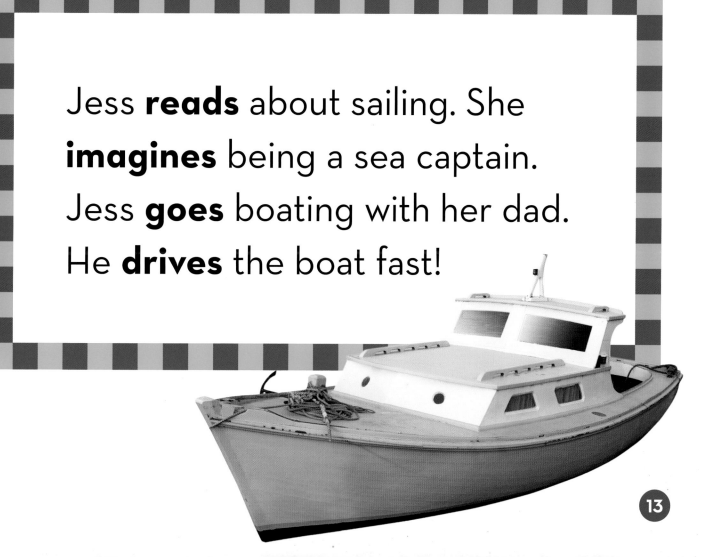

Tristan **competes** in a race. First he **swims**. Then he **bikes**. Then he **runs**. Everyone **tries** hard.

Did you find these verbs?

be	pulls
bikes	reads
bounce	run
build	runs
chases	sees
chomping	stands
competes	swims
drives	throw
eat	transform
goes	tries
imagines	walks
kick	watches
laughs	wiggles
plays	

To Learn More

IN THE LIBRARY

Cook, Julia. *It's Hard to Be a Verb!* Chattanooga, TN: National Center for Youth Issues, 2008.

Johnson, Robin. *The Word Wizard's Book of Verbs.* New York: Crabtree, 2015.

Malaspina, Ann. *Vivian and Victor Learn about Verbs.* Chicago: Norwood House, 2015.

ON THE WEB

Visit our Web site for links about verbs: **childsworld.com/links**

Note to Parents, Teachers, and Librarians: We routinely verify our Web links to make sure they are safe and active sites. So encourage your readers to check them out!